I0776835

A Brief History of the Order of the Eastern Star

by Charlotte O. Steber

with an introduction by "Black Books"

This work contains material that was originally published in 1917.

This publication is within the Public Domain.

*This edition is reprinted for entertainment purposes
and in accordance with all applicable Federal and International Laws.*

Introduction Copyright 2017 by Black Books

CREDITS & ACKNOWLEDGEMENTS

Front Cover
Black Books interpretation of the Order of the Eastern Star Logo.
(NOTE : This is NOT the actual OES Official logo, just our artist's
rendition. The actual logo is under copyright to the OES)

Back Cover
Author Charlotte O. Steber
from book interior.

Black Books Logo
Candle Collection by VectorPocket, via FreePik.com
Vanitas [Painting] by Bartholomäus Bruyn the Elder, Public Domain
Marbled Pedestal with Old Books by Kues1, via FreePik.com

Research / Sources
Wikimedia Commons
www.Commons.Wikimedia.org

Many thanks to all the incredible photographers, artists,
researchers, and archivists who share their great work.

PLEASE NOTE :
As with all reprinted books of this age that are intended to perfectly reproduce the
original edition, considerable pains and effort had to be undertaken to correct fading and
sometimes outright damage to existing proofs of this title. At times, this task can be quite
monumental, requiring an almost total rebuilding of some pages from digital proofs of
multiple copies. Despite this, imperfections still sometimes exist in the final proof and
may detract slightly from the visual appearance of the text.

DISCLAIMER :
Due to the age of this book, some methods or practices may have been deemed unsafe or
unacceptable in the interim years. In utilizing the information herein, you do so at your
own risk. We republish antiquarian books without judgment or revisionism, solely for
their historical and cultural importance, and for educational purposes.

Introduction

Black Books are pleased to present to you *A Brief History of the Order of the Eastern Star*, written by Charlotte O. Steber in 1917.

The Order of the Eastern Star is an appendant of the Freemasons, which is open to the female relatives of Master Masons. It was founded in 1876 by Dr. Robert Morris. The motto of the order is "*Charity, Faith and Loving Kindness.*"

Morris's idea behind the concept of the order – one of the few that allows both men and women as members – was so that the female relatives of the Master Masons could share in the "benefits of knowledge and self-improvement," that had always been available to all men who were part of the masonic family, according to the Order's website.

Morris's concept for a character-building masonic order was inspired by the stories biblical characters Adah, Ruth, Esther, Martha and Electa. Morris conceived the idea for the order while house-bound with sickness for a spell in 1850.

Although the Order's teachings are based on the Bible, the order is open to members of any and all faiths.

This is a fascinating glimpse into the history of this unusual masonic order, and an essential addition to the libraries of all masonic scholars and historians who study Freemasonry.

~ *Black Books*

¶ To the present and past Worthy Matrons of the Order of the Eastern Star, those noble and unselfish women—each of whom has given up several years of her life to help build up this beautiful Order and to spread its light of Charity, Truth and Loving Kindness — this little volume is dedicated.   ::   ::   ::

Charlotte O. Steber

INDEX TO CHAPTERS

WHAT IS HISTORY

Histories are as perfect as the historian is wise, and is gifted with an eye and a soul.—Carlyle.

¶ HISTORY is defined as a systematic written account of events, particularly of those affecting a nation, institution, science, or art, and usually connected with a philosophical explanation of their causes.

If all the important events that constitute the history of a country or of an institution or society were set down carefully and accurately as they occur, history would be written as it takes place and would be comparatively simple and accurate. But such is not the case. Let any person attempt to trace his or her ancestry back for a number of generations and he will immediately find what obstacles are in the path of the historian. Families do not keep a careful written record of all marriages and births. They are often so careless in these matters that in after years the exact date of birth is in doubt. And when an effort is made to follow out the collateral branches of the family we are soon lost in a labyrinth of unrecorded facts, and we arrive at points where we can trace back no farther.

So it is with the histories of nations, of cities, of institutions of all kinds. Whoever has delved into religion — who has investigated the history of the Septuagint and the Vulgate, as well as the myriad of other documents, including the many apocryphal writings — has discovered the same conditions.

EVOLUTION

Manners with fortunes,
Humors turn with climes,
Tenets with books,
And principles with times.
—A. Pope.

¶ BUT whatever subject is given to historic research we always find that the general principles of evolution have been followed. The first automobile was an ordinary wagon equipped with a crude motor. Gradually changes were made — shapes were made different — body, springs, wheels — all the important parts were changed in shape and construction to conform to their new environments until we have the finished motorcar of today — simply a development of evolution.

THE HISTORIAN

For truth has such a face and such a mien
As to be loved needs only to be seen.
                                    —*J. Dryden.*

❧ THE HISTORIAN is usually a compiler of information. Sometimes he knows a little about the current history of his subject, but usually the greater part of his history is a carefully put together assemblage of facts which he has gathered together from all the sources of knowledge on the subject at his command.

The accuracy of the history depends, therefore, very much on the thoroughness of the historian, on the knowledge that he is able to gather, and on his good judgment in separating the "fish stories" from the facts.

ORDER OF THE EASTERN STAR

Who soweth good seed shall surely reap;
The year grows rich as it groweth old,
And life's latest sands are its sands of gold.
—J. C. R. Dorr.

¶ THE ORDER OF THE EASTERN STAR as it now exists in the United States is composed of local Chapters which are organized into State jurisdictions called Grand Chapters. All of these Grand Chapters (more than fifty in 1917), except New York and New Jersey, have united together under the jurisdiction of a National organization known as the General Grand Chapter. This General Grand Chapter was organized in Indianapolis, Ind., on November 16, 1876, and the Rev. Willis D. Engle, the man who was most influential in bringing this about——who was a member of this first general body, helped to organize it, and was its first R. W. Grand Secretary — is still living at Indianapolis, Ind., and has written a splendid history of the Order, which, together with a very clear, concise and well-written brief history by Mrs. Sarah H. Terry, Grand Secretary of Kentucky, as well as various Masonic Encyclopedias, reports of proceedings, and other publications, have been the principal sources of information to the writer of this brief sketch.

In tracing back the history of the Order the writer feels that the principal element of confusion comes from not sufficiently taking into consideration the principles of evolution. To represent this idea let us again refer to the automobile. We might be able to find the man who first put a motor into a wagon and made it run the wagon. We could hardly call him the inventor of the modern automobile, which is the product of evolution, and represents the ideas and improvements of many men. So in a general way it is with the Order of the Eastern Star.

THE FUNDAMENTAL IDEA

*The light that lies
In Woman's eyes.
—T. Moore.*

¶ THE FUNDAMENTAL IDEA of this Order is an organization composed of the female relatives of Masons. Therefore, in looking up its history all organizations of female relatives of Masons must be taken into consideration. As the history of Masonry itself is shrouded in mystery and lost in the shadows of the past, it is plain to see that the history of women's organizations connected therewith must also be.

Our first reliable information on this subject of the organization of the women relatives of Masons seems to take us to what has been called "Androgynous Masonry" and "Adoptive Masonry." The word "Androgynous" is derived from two Greek words signifying "man" and "woman," and refers to an organization composed of men and women. This was simply a general term.

THE ADOPTIVE RITE

Little deeds of kindness
Little words of love,
Make our earth an Eden
Like the heaven above.
—J. A. Carney.

¶ IT APPEARS that during the eighteenth century — some authorities saying from about 1730 — Adoptive Masonry was established in France. It was called "Adoptive" because under its rules it was necessary for each Lodge to be placed under the charge of and held under the sanction and warrant of some regularly constituted Masonic Lodge, whose Master should be the presiding officer, assisted by a woman President. Each Lodge being thus adopted by some Masonic Lodge, it was called "Adoptive Masonry" or the

"Adoptive Rite."   The initiation ceremonies were not like Masonry, and it does not appear that the degrees or work corresponded with the work of the present Eastern Star — the only reason why it is an ancestor or predecessor being the fact that it was "Androgynous Masonry."   The author of "La Vraie Maconnerie d'Adoption," printed in 1787, who has given the best ritual of the Rite, thus briefly sums up the objects of the Institution:

"The first degree contains only, as it ought, moral ideas of Masonry; the second is the initiation into the first mysteries, commencing with the sin of Adam and concluding with the Ark of Noah as the first favor which God granted to men; the third and fourth are merely a series of types and figures drawn from the Holy Scriptures, by which we explain to the candidate the virtues which she ought to practice."

Considerable has been written to intimate and suggest that this French organization was brought here during Revolutionary times, but there seems to be no authentic history to substantiate such a conclusion. It is probably not true.

It is more than probable, however, that some people who had knowledge of these ceremonies in Europe came to this country and that their knowledge helped to create and bring into use some of the lectures which preceded the formation of the Eastern Star organization.

THE BEGINNINGS IN AMERICA

How many things by season seasoned are
To their right praise and true perfection?
—Shakespeare — Merchant of Venice.

❡ IT SEEMS that during the first half of the eighteenth century there was a demand for side degres and quite a horde sprang into existence and were conferred on the ladies promiscuously. Some of these are still in existence, and by various methods and authors were extensively used. Chief among them were "Ladies' Masonry," "Holy Virgin," "Ladies' Friend," "Kindred Degree," "Ark and Dove," "Good Samaritan," "Heroines of Jericho," "Maids of Jerusalem," "Daughters of Zion," "Daughters of Bethlehem," "Ladies of the Cross," and so on — all of which, perhaps, bore some analogy to the Eastern Star.

In his "Collection of Historic Papers Relating to the Eastern Star" Brother Alonzo J. Burton of New York says: "The Order made its appearance in the Colonies (New York City) in 1778, and it is safe to assume that it is a French importation." Brother Burton also quotes extensively from a Ritual called "Thesauros of the Ancient and Honorable Order of the Eastern Star," which purports to have been made in 1793. The author of this brief sketch after careful and exhaustive research is forced to the conclusion that the first statement is absolutely without foundation in fact, except in a very indirect manner as before stated; and as to the "Thesauros," there is absolutely not a scintilla of corroborative evidence, and the only logical conclusion is that it is a spurious publication. It is inconceivable that a society should have existed with a real organization from 1793 and that between that time and 1850 it should be impossible to find a single human being who ever belonged to it or knew of it as an organization.

MORRIS AND MACOY

Distinct as the billows, yet one as the sea.
—J. Montgomery.

¶ MUCH of our early history of the Order seems to center around two men — Robert Morris and Robert Macoy. Mrs. Sarah H. Terry, Grand Secretary of Kentucky, in her brief history of the Order, says:

"The history of the Eastern Star is divided into three eras — the first extending from 1850 to 1866, under the leadership of Dr. Rob. Morris, Poet Laureate of Kentucky Masonry; the second era from 1866 to 1876, under the leadership of Robert Macoy of New York: and the third era from 1876 to the present time, the one most noted for its growth and general development.

Of these eras the first is, perhaps, the most important, as it was a forerunner of and prepared the way for the later development. It is also noted as being the first Order of Androgynous degrees that was universally popular.

The real origin of the Order of the Eastern Star seems to have been shrouded in mystery by those claiming to be the founders. But that it is the outgrowth of an Order styling itself "The Rite of Adoption," which had its origin in France about 1780, is the most prevalent idea among some people.

Whatever the idea of the French was in giving to the ladies the various "Adoptive Rite" degrees, it has nothing to do with the American version of

Androgynous Masonry. There was **no** rite or ceremony of lasting merit until the American version came into vogue, and its American conception is not denied by many.

THE REAL ORIGIN OF THE EASTERN STAR

To make a happy fireside clime
*   To weans and wife,*
That's the true pathos and sublime
*   Of human life.*
                        —R. Burns.

¶ WHATEVER the inception, and whatever the use to which the Androgynous degrees were put, it remained for Dr. Rob. Morris to arrange the Eastern Star.

Mr. Morris had traveled much and had written many books on Masonry which were used as text and reference books. He had taken Masonry from the farcical methods into which it had fallen and had clothed it with divine and symbolic meaning, Biblical lore, and historical research.

He was never quite satisfied that all the good in Masonry should be confined to men. There was always in his mind the thought that Masonry should be for the entire family. By the laws of that ancient Order women are not eligible to its degrees. First, because of the age in which Masonry originated. Woman at that time was in a low state of social development; by custom she was man's inferior and by habit submissive to all the restraint of tradition and race. Second, because by the operative methods of Masons she was considered too fragile to undertake the tasks of men engaged in heavy work, no matter how well organized or arranged.

But Masonry had been removed from this embryonic state and had become both operative and speculative.

Although Dr. Morris knew that he would not dare change the ancient landmarks of the Order, his mind set to work on some method by which women could share with the Masonic brother the same inspiration that prompts man to noble deeds.

While this idea had been uppermost in his mind for some time, it was not till 1850, while confined to his home from the effects of an accident, that he evolved and fully developed the Eastern Star.

For years, practically speaking during the first era, Dr. Morris and many prominent Masons gave these lectures and "secrets" and "mysteries," which were discussed behind closed doors and in whispers long afterwards. There was no organization, however; yet the story was so firmly planted in the minds of the enlightened that the story, signs, and passes were more or less accurately remembered.

Dr. Morris continued writing during all this period and many books and manuals came from his hands. The Mosaic Book (1855), the Monitor, later the Sorosis, and finally the Morris Manual (1860), and many others were added to his collection.

In his history Rev. Willis D. Engle quotes freely from books, letters, and other matter written by Dr. Morris, and seems to very fully establish the proposition that Morris evolved the Eastern Star either from his own ideas, or from the ideas that had been already planted but were of such short life that nothing came of them. And it is plain that to

Dr. Morris and his untiring efforts we owe the Eastern Star as we have it in its present form.

This bit of history from the pen of Mrs. Terry seems to be squarely and thoughtfully stated.

ROBERT MORRIS

I want to help you to grow as beautiful as God meant you to be when he thought of you first.
—George MacDonald.

¶ ROBERT MORRIS himself at one time said in "The Voice of Masonry":

"My first regular course of lectures was given in November, 1850, at Colliersville, Tennessee. . . . At Colliersville likewise I conferred the degrees of the Eastern Star and Good Samaritan. Both of these I had received some years before, the latter by Brother Stevens, the same who presided at my passing and raising. The restrictions under which the Eastern Star was communicated to me were that it should only be given to Master Masons,

their wives, widows, sisters and daughters, and only when five or more ladies
of the classes named were present;
these rules I have always adhered to."

Willis D. Engle in his history says:

"After reviewing all the facts it must
be concluded that Brother Morris did
not originate the Ritual of the Order,
but that, receiving the degrees by com-
munication, as above stated, and taking
the Ritual as used before he took up
the occupation of a Masonic lecturer,
he embellished and adorned it, and
started the Order toward systematic
organization. Certainly as it at present
exists in this country, Brother Morris
was the master builder, and that ought
to be enough glory, without his claiming or having ascribed to him the orig-
ination of the degree, which is still often
done by those holding high official posi-

tions in the Order — even in the General Grand Chapter."

It is therefore evident that he did not originate the whole thing. It is beyond question, however, as both of these eminent authorities agree, that he became interested in this subject at an important period in the evolution of "Androgynous Masonry," and it is sure that he revised and formulated the matter, and did more than any other person to bring it into prominence from 1850 until after the close of the Civil War.

CONSTELLATIONS

When night hath set her silver lamp on high.
Then is the time for study.—P. J. Bailey.

¶ IT APPEARS that Robert Morris was born near Boston, Mass., August 31, 1818, and died July 31, 1888. He is buried at Lagrange, Kentucky, and an Eastern Star is engraved upon his tomb. He lived during much of his life in Mississippi, Tennessee and Kentucky. He became a Mason at Oxford, Miss., March 5, 1846, and received the Eastern Star degrees in lecture form in 1848 or 1849, and in 1850, while residing at Jackson, Miss., he systematized said degrees with the idea of giving them more organic form. He continued to confer the degrees, and in 1855 inaugurated a Supreme Constellation, claiming that "no such attempt upon a national basis has heretofore been made in America." The Mosaic Book issued by Morris stated that

"The Supreme Constellation was, at the organization of the Rite, a self-assumed body, and will so continue during a period sufficiently protracted to test the merits of the American Adoptive Rite, and afford experience as a basis of its improvement."

Robert Morris became the "Most Enlightened Grand Luminary" in this organization, and charters were issued in many parts of the United States. It will be noted that although each individual constellation became a bona fide organization, the Supreme Constellation was self-appointed.

FAMILIES

This world is not for aye,
Nor 'tis not strange
That even our loves
Should with our fortunes change.
Shakespeare — Hamlet.

¶ IN 1860, for some reason, the constellation form of organization was discontinued and charters were issued for the organization of "Families," with Robert Morris still as "M. E. Grand Luminary." Quite a number of "Families" were thus chartered between 1860 and 1868 in various parts of the country. This "Family" organization immediately preceded the Chapter organization, and in a few instances "Families" were reorganized and renamed, like Friendship Family No. 103 of Brooklyn, which was chartered January 25, 1866, and was reorganized as Esther Chapter No. 2 in June, 1869. Also Miriam Family No. 111, chartered October 6, 1866, and reorganized as Miriam Chapter No. 1 of Chicago on March 4, 1869. Mrs. Lorraine J. Pitkin, the R. W. Grand Secretary of the present General Grand Chapter, was a member of this "Family."

CHAPTERS

From lower to the higher next,
Not to the top, is Nature's text.
                        —*J. R. Lowell.*

¶ MOST of the "Constellations" and "Families" that had been chartered died out, however, and became lost in a historical sense. It was in 1867 and 1868 that Robert Macoy of New York developed a Ritual with initiatory and other ceremonies for the organization of Chapters, and from this time dates the organization of Chapters. In considering the period that Mrs. Terry designates as the second era, from 1866 to 1876, it is necessary to appreciate one fundamental fact: Up to this time there was no real general organization, either State or National. The various charters that were issued under the Morris regime as well as those under the Macoy control were issued by self-appointed and self-constituted general organizations which amounted to little more than the absolute personal ownership of those men. The charters, rituals and other matter were sold and it was a purely business transaction. The money received for them went into private purses, not into the treasury of a general organization of which all local bodies were a part. The real true organization ended in every case with the local itself, as there was no governmental organization which it helped to make and of which it formed a part. It was for this reason principally that during the first era it did not become a real organization.

REAL ORGANIZATION

Man yields to custom, as he bows to fate,
In all things ruled—mind, body, and estate.
—G. Crabbe.

¶ DURING the second era, however, this fundamental principle of true organization developed. The Chapter system, together with the more friendly coöperation of Masonry itself, as well as other causes, began to mold the Eastern Star into a real Order. The Chapters began to unite in the different States, forming true general bodies composed of representatives of all the local bodies, and perfecting organizations with which all members and locals were directly and inseparably affiliated. That the Chapter system was not the sole cause of this new era is proven conclusively in Michigan and Indiana. In Michigan a "Grand Lodge of Adoptive Masonry" was organized at Adrian October 30, 1867, by sixty delegates representing fifteen Lodges. And in Indiana a "Grand Lodge of Adoptive Masonry" was organized at Elkhart January 27, 1869. Both of these Grand Lodges were built out of organizations that grew from the Morris teachings and had as their basis what is known as the "Tatem Ritual," which was put together by Mr. John H. Tatem of Michigan. This Indiana Grand Lodge had another meeting and then went out of existence. The Michigan Grand Lodge, however, continued, and the present Grand Chapter of Michigan is this very organization with such changes in Ritual and names as became necessary in 1878, when it joined the

General Grand Chapter of the Eastern Star. Mr. Engle in his history says of this:

"The Order in Michigan, by cheerfully giving up its old work, which had many points of beauty and appropriateness not embodied in the General Grand Chapter Ritual, and relinquishing its form of organization, which antedated that of the Chapter form by at least a year, and its Grand Lodge organization being nearly three years older than the oldest Grand Chapter, for the sake of union and uniformity, certainly demonstrated its title to the prosperity that has crowned its later years."

It is thus apparent that the Michigan Grand Chapter is beyond question the oldest "Eastern Star Grand Body" in existence.

THE FIRST CHAPTER

He spake, and into every heart his words
Carried new strength and courage.
                              —Homer — Iliad.

¶ TO RETURN to Robert Macoy and the beginning of the Chapter system: In December, 1866, a great Masonic fair was held in New York City to aid the Masonic Hall and Home fund. At this fair quite a number of ladies — relatives of the Masons—took part. These ladies had all received the Eastern Star degrees which had been given quite frequently in lecture form at Masonic Lodge entertainments for several years preceding this time. After the fair, on January 21, 1867, they organized a society and called themselves "Sisters of the Eastern Star." Robert Macoy, who was a publisher of works on Masonry and Adoptive Masonry, attended these meetings and conferred the degrees in lecture form. During 1867 and 1868 he formulated a Chapter Ritual, and on December 28, 1868, this organization became Alpha Chapter No. 1, under a Macoy charter, and its members became familiarly known as the "Alpha Sisters." This form of organization soon spread and Mr. Macoy issued charters in various parts of the United States and also in foreign countries during the next few years.

In the same manner as Brother Morris had constituted himself "M. E. Grand Luminary" over his Constellation and Family systems, Brother Macoy now constituted himself "National Grand Secretary" over his newly formulated Chapter system, and afterwards assumed the title of "Supreme Grand Patron." It can readily be seen that at this stage in the evolution of the Eastern Star the efforts of Brothers Morris and Macoy were logical and helped wonderfully to spread it. But as the individual Chapters began to multiply, the fire of true governmental organization began to spread.

GRAND CHAPTERS

Our acts our angels are, or good or ill.
Our fatal shadows that walk by us still.
                                                    —J. Fletcher.

❡ ON JULY 18, 1870, the three Chapters of the State of New Jersey organized a Grand Chapter. On November 3, 1870, representatives from fourteen of the twenty Chapters then in existence in New York met and organized the Grand Chapter of New York. And gradually year by year all the States where the Order had spread organized Grand Chapters.

By 1874 many Chapters were organized and Grand Chapters formed, and there was strong talk of organizing a Supreme or General Grand Chapter.

GENERAL GRAND CHAPTER

Good nature and good sense must ever join;
To err is human, to forgive divine.
—A. Pope.

¶ THE FIRST definite proposition to strike at the root of the matter and put everything upon a reasonable basis by forming a legitimate supreme body, was made by Willis D. Engle in the New York Courier of August 30, 1874, as follows:

"Two things, it seems to me, are needed immediately: first, a Supreme Grand Chapter composed of representatives from the several Grand Chapters; second, revision and general boiling down and finishing up of the Ritual, which is now defective, both in style and language. Let us all buckle on our armor and enter in earnest on the work of improving and extending the Order, and a very few years will place it in a very enviable position."

Brother Engle continued the agitation of this subject, writing to all the prominent people in the Order in reference to it. Its organization is undoubtedly due to his efforts more than to those of any other person.

Finally the Grand Chapter of Indiana became urgent in the matter, and after many drawbacks, at last sent out an appeal for a General Council for the discussion of this subject, and at its meeting in April, 1876, adopted resolutions and recommendations and mailed them to each Grand Chapter then in existence. All the Grand Chapters being notified, this General Council was called together November 15,

1876, in Indianapolis, and to this delegates from the various Grand Chapters were sent, and the organization known thereafter as the General Grand Chapter, Order of the Eastern Star, was organized, with Mrs. Elizabeth Butler as the first Most Worthy Grand Matron; Rev. J. D. Vencil, Most Worthy Grand Patron, and Rev. W. E. Engle, Right Worthy Grand Secretary.

The General Grand Chapter has control of the Ritual, secret work and labyrinth, and these can be obtained only through them. This constitutes the principal source of revenue for the General Grand Chapter. Dr. Morris was not a member of the first General Grand Chapter, but was later made an honorary member.

The officers of this body are elected triennially, and are usually promoted from the Associate Grand Conductress up to Most Worthy Grand Matron. The Right Worthy Grand Secretary has never been changed but once, when Mrs. Lorraine J. Pitkin succeeded Brother Engle. The Grand Secretary's office is at 1066 Berwyn Avenue, Chicago, Ill.

It is fast becoming the custom of the Grand Chapters to do likewise, and the one elected Associate Grand Conductress is promoted annually until she is Worthy Grand Matron, the Secretaries being continued in office when efficient and willing.

Since its organization the General Grand Chapter has been self-supporting. It is the only National organization which has been financially successful without a per capita tax from its constituent members. The expenses allowed the Most Worthy Grand officers, the salary of the Right Worthy Grand Secretary, as well as office rent and other expenses have been paid by the ample amount taken in, and there is besides a sum of many thousand dollars now in the treasury of this body.

It has its own laws, and its own regulations and landmarks. It is the duty of this body to see that no laws of any Grand jurisdiction conflict with its own, and yet every Grand jurisdiction has the right to have its own laws and government. This leads to various differences, but chiefly in minor interpretations. The Ritual has been revised slightly since its first adoption, the last revision having been made since the 1913 session, when it was authorized, and is now considered perfect, so far as the work is concerned, and is used by all the Grand jurisdictions, New York and New Jersey excepted.

The New York Ritual has been revised several times, and Dr. Albert H. Brundage of Brooklyn, who has had charge of the last revision, says: "No effort has been spared to make it grammatically and historically correct, comprehensive, clear and direct in statement, anticipatory of and truly serviceable for difficult or emergent situation — in short, to make it a reliable textbook and guide." New York members believe that their Ritual is beyond question the best.

NEW YORK GRAND CHAPTER

To heal divisions, to relieve the oppressed,
In virtue rich; in blessing others, blessed.
—Homer.

¶ NEW YORK STATE did not participate in the organization of the General Grand Chapter. As was before noted, the first Eastern Star organization to come into existence as a Chapter, and consequently the very beginning of the Chapter system, was Alpha No. 1 of New York, on December 28, 1868. This started under a Macoy charter and with a Macoy Ritual. New York State was also practically the first to organize a Grand Chapter (November 3, 1870). Although New Jersey was technically first, it was organized with only three Chapters, and they were in reality direct offshoots from the New York organization. For various reasons Brother Macoy was unfriendly to the organization of the General Grand Chapter, and as during the first few years of the existence of the Order in New York State his influence was very great, New York remained aloof.

Many of the pioneer members in New York became imbued with the idea that New York being the place where the Chapter system originated, should not be superseded by an organization that came later. They regarded it as a sort of usurpation. The New York Grand Chapter has therefore continued alone, supreme in itself. It has prospered splendidly and has today (1917) something more than 500 Chapters, with a membership of about 60,000, which is greater than that of any other State except Illinois and possibly Michigan. Illinois has several thousand more members, and the figures in Michigan are very nearly the same as those of New York. As Michigan is much smaller in population, it seems to be the banner Eastern Star State in point of membership.

The New York Grand Chapter has established a beautiful Home and Infirmary at Oriskany, which was dedicated September 3, 1916. Previous to this for quite a number of years a splendid Home had been maintained at Waterville, which was discontinued upon the completion of the Oriskany Home. The New York Grand Chapter also has a large sum in its treasury and is probably the most prosperous and substantial Eastern Star organization in existence. It has been legally incorporated, has adopted and patented a distinctive emblem, and in every way commands the respect and confidence of the members and of the community at large. It maintains beautiful offices at 30 East 42nd Street, New York City, where the Grand Secretary can at all times be found and where the members and Chapters can at all times obtain any needed information in reference to the affairs of the Order.

Looking at the subject in a broad light, it seems rather strange that New York and New Jersey did not also become affiliated with the General Grand Chapter. That such a result was contemplated by those who organized the New York Grand Chapter on November 3, 1870, is conclusively proven by the fact that in the first New York State Constitution, adopted on said date, in

Section 4 of Article 1, entitled "Powers," is found this expression, referring to the powers of the Grand Chapter of New York which was then organized: "It has power to exercise all the rights of sovereignty within the limits of its jurisdiction, subject to the provisions of its own Constitution, and the Constitution of the Supreme Grand Chapter of the United States."

Yet in November, 1876, when the General Grand Chapter was formed, New York State did not participate. In the 1877 New York State proceedings we find this reference: "Brother M. T. Webb, Grand Patron, took a stand against the formation of a General Grand Chapter, but Brother J. M. Hopper, who was elected Grand Patron, seemed to favor such a body, or, at least, asked that the question be thoroughly considered. During the meeting a resolution was introduced and tabled to send delegates to the General Grand Chapter." And in the 1878 New York State proceedings a motion to take this resolution from the table was lost.

To be sure, having lived apart for years, New York in particular never having been connected with the General Grand Chapter, it is logical that there should be many apparent reasons why they should not give up their complete independence. Of course, the Order is to all intents and purposes one great organization, the relationship of the Grand bodies is the most cordial and friendly, and exchanges of courtesies and recognition of membership takes place substantially the same as though all were united.

CHANGES

*Weep not that the world changes—did it keep
A stable, changeless state, it were cause indeed
to weep.   —W. C. Bryant.*

¶ IN THE GENERAL EVOLUTION of the Order a number of changes may be noted. For example, at first the Grand Patron was the principal officer. In New York State this was so until 1885. In the early years it was called the "Adoptive Rite," and this carried with it the idea of immediate and close relationship with some Masonic Lodge. This made it in a sense what might be termed "Female Masonry," and was obnoxious to many Masons. Evolution has completely eliminated this idea. The terms "Adoptive Rite" or "Adoptive Masonry" are entirely misleading, as they do not in any manner apply to the Order of the Eastern Star as it now exists. As an organization it is entirely independent and free from the Masonic Order, but as its members must be Masons or relatives of Masons, its personnel is of necessity completely Masonic.

A GRAND OBJECT

That man may last but never lives,
Who much receives but nothing gives;
Whom none can love, whom none can thank.
Creation's blot, creation's blank.
—T. Gibbons.

¶ THE NECESSITY of having an object in view for the promotion of united labor, and the urgent needs for such labor, led the Grand Chapters to take up the idea of establishing either funds for homes already built, or hospital funds, but more lasting has been the idea of the Eastern Star Home, of which many Grand Chapters now boast. Some of the Grand Chapters work hand in hand with the Masons and assist in all ways possible in the maintenance of their Homes. Others have infirmaries or wards, while many have Homes of their own, supported and directed by themselves. In all Grand Chapters we find a neat sum for charitable purposes.

SPREAD OF THE ORDER

Eternal process moving on,
From state to state the spirit moves.
—A. Tennyson.

¶ IN ADDITION to the Grand Chapters throughout the United States, Grand Chapters have also been established in British Columbia, Ontario, Alberta, Saskatchewan, and Porto Rico within the last few years, and there are good prospects for one in Alaska. There is also a Grand Chapter in Scotland, but relations have been severed between it and the General Grand Chapter. Local Chapters have also been organized in Quebec, New Brunswick, Manitoba, and Yukon, in the Panama Canal Zone, Cuba, Mexico, the Philippine Islands and in the

Hawaiian Islands. The total membership of the Order in 1917 is 819,724.

This is composed of 740,291 under the jurisdiction of the General Grand Chapter and 79,433 not under its jurisdiction, of which the New York State Grand Chapter controls about 60,000. Every State in the Union now has a Grand Chapter except Delaware. The Order of the Eastern Star is the largest women's organization in the world, and in point of membership ranks fifth among the largest fraternal organizations in America.

CHARITY, TRUTH, AND LOVING KINDNESS

Blessed are they which do hunger and thirst after righteousness: for they shall be filled.—Matthew v:6.

¶ MASONRY alone has stood unique among the institutions of men, the patron and parent of all organizations fraternal. The Order of the Eastern Star holds a similar relation to similar orders. Some may seek to change it to suit the whims of time and place, but this Order, built on all that is elemental in good character, emphasizes those virtues which lie at the root of all well-thinking, and from which spring all rectitude of conduct.

The Order seems to be established on a firm basis. With Charity, Truth, and Loving Kindness for its motto, it ought to sanctify every home that it enters. It stands as a bright monument to female secrecy and fidelity, and may it ever shine to lighten woman's pathway till time shall be no more.